JOHN STOTT BIBLE STUDIES

12 Studies with Commentary for Individuals or Groups

D1498668

1 Timothy & Titus

Fighting the Good Fight

John
STOTT

with Lin Johnson

Inter-Varsity Press
Nottingham, England

IVP Connect
An imprint of InterVarsity Press
Downers Grove, Illinois

InterVarsity Press, USA
P.O. Box 1400, Downers Grove, IL 60515-1426, USA
World Wide Web: www.ivpress.com
Email: email@ivpress.com

Inter-Varsity Press, England
Norton Street, Nottingham NG7 3HR, England
Website: www.ivpbooks.com
Email: ivp@ivpbooks.com

InterVarsity Press®, USA, is the book-publishing division of InterVarsity Christian Fellowship/USA®, a student movement active on campus at hundreds of universities, colleges and schools of nursing in the United States of America, and a member movement of the International Fellowship of Evangelical Students. For information about local and regional activities, write Public Relations Dept., InterVarsity Christian Fellowship/USA, 6400 Schroeder Rd., P.O. Box 7895, Madison, WI 53707-7895, or visit the IVCF website at <www.intervarsity.org>.

Inter-Varsity Press, England, is closely linked with the Universities and Colleges Christian Fellowship, a student movement connecting Christian Unions in universities and colleges throughout Great Britain, and a member movement of the International Fellowship of Evangelical Students. Website: www.uccf.org.uk.

All Scripture quotations, unless otherwise indicated, are taken from the Holy Bible, New International Version®. NIV®. Copyright © 1973, 1978, 1984 by International Bible Society. Used by permission of Zondervan Publishing House. Distributed in the U.K. by permission of Hodder and Stoughton Ltd. All rights reserved. "NIV" is a registered trademark of International Bible Society. UK trademark number 1448790.

This study guide is based on and includes excerpts adapted from Guard the Truth ©1996 by John R. W. Stott.

Design: Cindy Kiple
Images: malcolm romain/iStockphoto

USA ISBN 978-0-8308-2167-9
UK ISBN 978-1-84474-321-6

Printed in the United States of America ∞

P   23   22   21   20   19   18   17   16   15   14   13   12   11   10   9   8   7   6   5   4   3

Y   27   26   25   24   23   22   21   20   19   18   17   16   15   14   13   12   11

Introducing 1 Timothy & Titus

Visit most Christian bookstores, and you'll find a variety of plaques and posters that summarize biblical truth in pithy statements. For example:

"Truth not translated into life is dead truth."

"The greatest homage we can pay to truth is to use it."

Both of these statements by anonymous authors are apt summaries of Paul's letters to Timothy and Titus.

These letters, along with 2 Timothy, are often called "the Pastoral Epistles" because they are concerned with the pastoral care and oversight of local churches. Paul addresses six main topics that he wants Timothy to relate to the churches.

☐ How to keep *doctrine* uncorrupted by false teaching.

☐ The role of *public worship* along with the roles of men and women in the conduct of it.

☐ The conditions of eligibility for *pastors,* elders and deacons.

☐ Instructions for *local leadership,* especially younger leaders.

☐ The church's *social responsibility* to widows, elders and slaves.

☐ The church's attitude toward *material possessions.*

The three chapters of Titus relate to the three main contexts of Christian living, namely the church, the home and the world. In all three, Paul emphasized the relationship between doctrine and duty, belief and behavior.

Getting to Know Timothy

Most readers find Timothy a very congenial character. We feel that he is one of us in all our frailty. A halo would not have fitted comfortably on his head. No, the evidence is plain that he was a real human being like us, with all the infirmity and vulnerability which that entails. To begin with, he was still comparatively young when Paul addressed this letter to him (4:12)—in his midthirties, which was still within the limits of "youth." Second, he was temperamentally shy, needing affirmation, encouragement and reassurance (2 Timothy 1:7). Third, Timothy was physically infirm and suffered from a recurrent stomach problem (5:23).

Getting to Know Titus

Like Timothy, Titus was entrusted with the care of churches to complete what Paul had started. Titus was a Gentile believer whom Paul had led to the Lord. He accompanied Paul on his missionary journeys and spent time on special assignment in Corinth while Paul was elsewhere. Later Paul left him on the island of Crete where he received this letter with specific instructions about practicing truth.

Paul's letter to Titus has always been a popular little New Testament document, especially among Christian leaders who hold responsibility in the church. For although the letter is directed to Titus as an individual, it also looks beyond him to the churches he supervised. It does not require much imagination to sit down beside Titus to read Paul's letter as if it were addressed to us. For the apostle's instructions to his trusted lieutenant have extraordinary contemporary relevance.

A Message for Us

Let no one say that Scripture is out of date. In 1556 Calvin called 1 Timothy "highly relevant to our own times" (*The Epistles of Paul to Timothy and Titus,* p. 182). More than 400 years later we can make the same claim of both 1 Timothy and Titus. May your study of these letters expand your view of the church and grow you into spiritual maturity.

Suggestions for Individual Study

1. As you begin each study, pray that God will speak to you through his Word.

2. Read the introduction to the study and respond to the question that follows it. This is designed to help you get into the theme of the study.

3. The studies are written in an inductive format designed to help you discover for yourself what Scripture is saying. Each study deals with a particular passage so that you can really delve into the author's meaning in that context. Read and reread the passage to be studied. The questions are written using the language of the New International Version, so you may wish to use that version of the Bible. The New Revised Standard Version is also recommended.

4. Each study includes three types of questions. *Observation* questions ask about the basic facts: who, what, when, where and how. *Interpretation* questions delve into the meaning of the passage. *Application* questions (also found in the "Apply" section) help you discover the implications of the text for growing in Christ. These three keys unlock the treasures of Scripture.

Write your answers to the study questions in the spaces provided or in a personal journal. Writing can bring clarity and deeper understanding of yourself and of God's Word.

5. In the studies you will find some commentary notes designed to give help with complex verses by giving further biblical and cultural background and contextual information. The notes in the studies are not designed to answer the questions for you. They are to help you along as you learn to study the Bible for yourself. After you have worked through the questions and notes in the guide, you may want to read the accompanying commentary by John Stott in the Bible Speaks Today series. This will give you more information about the text.

6. Move to the "Apply" section. These questions will help you connect the key biblical themes to your own life. Putting the application into practice is one of the keys to growing in Christ.

7. Use the guidelines in the "Pray" section to focus on God, thanking him for what you have learned and praying about the applications that have come to mind.

Suggestions for Members of a Group Study

1. Come to the study prepared. Follow the suggestions for individual study mentioned above. You will find that careful preparation will greatly enrich your time spent in group discussion.

2. Be willing to participate in the discussion. The leader of your group will not be lecturing. Instead, she or he will be encouraging the members of the group to discuss what they have learned. The leader will be asking the questions that are found in this guide.

3. Stick to the topic being discussed. Your answers should be based on the verses which are the focus of the discussion and not on outside authorities such as commentaries or speakers. These studies focus on a particular passage of Scripture. Only rarely should you refer to other portions of the Bible. This allows for everyone to participate on equal ground and for in-depth study.

4. Be sensitive to the other members of the group. Listen attentively when they describe what they have learned. You may be surprised by their insights! Each question assumes a variety of answers. Many questions do not have "right" answers, particularly questions that aim at meaning or application. Instead the questions push us to explore the passage more thoroughly.

When possible, link what you say to the comments of others. Also, be affirming whenever you can. This will encourage some of the more hesitant members of the group to participate.

5. Be careful not to dominate the discussion. We are sometimes so eager to express our thoughts that we leave too little opportunity for others to respond. By all means participate! But allow others to also.

6. Expect God to teach you through the passage being discussed and through the other members of the group. Pray that you will have an enjoyable and profitable time together, but also that as a result of the study you will find ways that you can take action individually and/or as a group.

7. It will be helpful for groups to follow a few basic guidelines. These guidelines, which you may wish to adapt to your situation, should be read at the beginning of the first session.

☐ Anything said in the group is considered confidential and will not be discussed outside the group unless specific permission is given to do so.

☐ We will provide time for each person present to talk if he or she feels comfortable doing so.

☐ We will talk about ourselves and our own situations, avoiding conversation about other people.

☐ We will listen attentively to each other.

☐ We will be very cautious about giving advice.

8. If you are the group leader, you will find additional suggestions at the back of the guide.

1
TRUE OR FALSE?

1 Timothy 1:1-11

*T*ruth is not a valued commodity today. For example, lying to prevent personal embarrassment or to avoid hurting someone's feelings comes naturally to most of us. Advertisers regularly use deception to sell products. And few people teach and practice the truth of the Ten Commandments, let alone the rest of Scripture.

But the apostle Paul's overriding preoccupation throughout 1 Timothy—as well as the other pastoral letters of Titus and 2 Timothy—was with the truth, that it may be faithfully guarded and handed on. The relevance of this theme at the end of the twentieth century is evident. Contemporary culture is being overtaken and submerged by the spirit of postmodernism, which declares that there is no such thing as objective or universal truth; that all so-called truth is purely subjective, being culturally conditioned; and that therefore we all have our own truth, which has as much right to respect as anybody else's.

In contrast to this relativization of truth, it is wonderfully refreshing to read Paul's unambiguous commitment to it.

Open ——————————————————————

■ When is it difficult to practice God's truth instead of dishonesty and deception?

Study

■ *Read 1 Timothy 1:1-2.* Paul was expecting to visit Timothy in Ephesus soon and would then assume responsibility for the churches. But he seemed to have anticipated the possibility of being delayed and therefore sent Timothy these written instructions, so that during his absence Timothy would know how to regulate the life of the churches (3:14-15; 4:13). This letter, therefore, although addressed to Timothy personally, is not a private communication.

---

1. What do we learn about Paul from these opening verses?

---

2. What did Paul mean when he described Timothy as "my true son in the faith"?

---

3. What did Paul teach Timothy about God in this introduction?

Read 1 Timothy 1:3-7. The verb which Paul used both in 1:3 and 6:3 clearly indicates that there is a norm of doctrine from which the false teachers had deviated. It is called "the faith," "the truth," "the sound doctrine," "the teaching" and "the good deposit." In nearly every one of these expressions the noun is preceded by the definite article, indicating that already a body of doctrine existed which was an agreed standard by which all teaching could be tested and judged. It was the teaching of Christ and of his apostles.

---

4. What false teachings did Paul point out for Timothy?

5. What do verses 6 and 7 tell us about the nature and consequences of false teaching?

At this time there was some fanciful literature circulating in the Jewish world which rewrote sections of the Old Testament with embellishments and additions. It seems almost certain that the false teaching was primarily a Jewish aberration (Titus 1:10). They used the Old Testament law to fit their own conjectures. To Paul the whole approach was frivolous.

6. In contrast, the goal of true teaching is love. How do purity, a clean conscience and faith manifest themselves in love?

7. How can we live out the goal of love in a society characterized by false and empty teaching?

Summary: Paul paints a double contrast between speculation and faith in God's revelation and between controversy and love for one another. Here are two practical tests for us to apply to all teaching. The first is the test of faith: does it come from God, being in agreement with apostolic doctrine (so that it may be received by faith), or is it the product of fertile human imagination? The second is the test of love: does it promote unity in the body of Christ, or if not (since truth itself can divide), is it irresponsibly divisive? *Faith* means that we receive it from God; *love* means that it builds up the church. The ultimate criteria by which to judge any teaching are whether it promotes the glory of God and the good of the church.

8. *Read 1 Timothy 1:8-11.* In contrast to false teaching, Paul affirmed the right use of the law. What is it?

---

9. One body of absolute truth is the Ten Commandments, recorded in Exodus 20:1-17. The first six examples of law-breaking ("lawbreakers and rebels, the ungodly and sinful, the unholy and irreligious") clearly refer to our relationship with God, although they do not necessarily correspond with the first four commandments. How do the rest of these examples compare with the remainder of the Ten Commandments?

Commandment   **Law-Breakers**

---

10. Why is it so important to maintain sound doctrine and refute false teachings?

Summary: It is particularly noteworthy that sins which contradict the law (as breaches of the Ten Commandments) are also contrary to the sound doctrine of the gospel. So the moral standards of the gospel do not differ from the moral standards of the law. We must not therefore imagine that because we have embraced the gospel we may now contradict the law! To be sure, we have been released from the law's condemnation so that we are no longer "under" it in that sense. But God sent his Son to die for us and now puts his Spirit within us in order that the righteous requirement of the law may be fulfilled in us. There is no antithesis between law and gospel in the moral standards which they teach; the antithesis is in the way of salvation, since the law condemns, while the gospel justifies.

Apply

■ What false teachings do we have to guard against today? Identify several specific examples.

What can you do to increase your discernment between false and true teachings and to follow the truth?

Pray

■ Ask God for discernment to know whether the teachings you encounter are true or false and for the strength to follow the truth.

2
BELIEF THAT BEHAVES

1 Timothy 1:12-20

I lost fifty pounds on x, y, z diet plan."

"I now have a full head of hair thanks to this miracle hair grower."

"If you join our fitness program, you can have a body like this by summer."

The ads and commercials touting changes are hard to miss. Many companies sell their services and products with ads showing what people look like before and after. The Bible contains before and after stories too. In the second half of 1 Timothy 1, Paul wrote about himself and the gospel that had been entrusted to him. He retold the story of his conversion and commissioning, sandwiching it between praise to God. His whole life is permeated with thanksgiving, not only for his salvation but also for the privilege of having been made an apostle.

Open
■ Describe a person you know whose life has changed dramatically.

Study
1. *Read 1 Timothy 1:12-17.* Describe Paul before and after he became a believer.

2. For what did Paul thank God? Why?

---

3. Paul went on to quote the first of the five "trustworthy sayings" in the pastoral epistles. On each occasion the saying is pithy, almost proverbial, is perhaps a familiar quotation from an early hymn or creed, and is given by Paul his own apostolic endorsement. This first "faithful saying" is a concise summary of the gospel. What does it tell us about the gospel?

---

4. Why did Christ show Paul mercy?

---

5. How was Paul an example of Christ's "unlimited patience"?

---

6. What does the doxology in verse 17 tell you about Paul's relationship with God?

Summary: Although Paul had been a blasphemer and a violent persecutor, the grace of Christ had overwhelmed him. He received mercy partly because of his ignorant unbelief and partly in order to display for the benefit of future generations the limitless patience of Christ. It was this experience of Christ's grace, mercy and patience that provided the foundation of Paul's evangelistic enthusiasm. Just so, nobody can share the gospel with passion and power today who has not had a comparably personal experience of Christ.

7. *Read 1 Timothy 1:18-20.* What is the "good fight" Paul urged Timothy to fight (see also 6:12)?

---

8. What part do faith and a good conscience play in engaging in this battle?

---

9. Paul noted that some believers had shipwrecked their faith. Why would Christians do this?

---

10. Paul had handed Hymenaeus and Alexander over to Satan, excommunicating them. How could he do this?

Summary: Belief and behavior, conviction and conscience, the intellectual and the moral, are closely linked. This is because God's truth contains ethical demands. As Jesus said, "If anyone chooses to do God's will, he will find out [or "know"] whether my teaching comes form God" (John 7:17). In other words, doing is the key to discovering, obedience the key to assurance. By contrast, it is when people are determined to live in sin that they suppress the truth. So if we disregard the voice of conscience, allowing sin to remain unconfessed and unforsaken, our faith will not long survive.

Apply

■ How are you an example so others will believe in Christ?

In what areas do you need to change to be a better example?

What specific steps can you take to keep from shipwrecking your faith in Christ?

Pray

■ How has God shown you mercy? What difference has it made in your life? Spend a few minutes thanking God for his mercy and the results.

3
WORSHIP & WOMEN

1 Timothy 2

Christians attend church services for a variety of reasons. Some go to hear the preaching, some to see their friends, some out of a sense of duty or obligation, some for the music.

According to Paul, the primary reason for public gatherings is to worship God. Whenever we fail to take public worship seriously, we are less than the fully biblical Christians we claim to be. In consequence our worship services are slovenly, perfunctory, mechanical and dull or, in an attempt to remedy this, we go to the opposite extreme and become repetitive, unreflective and even flippant.

Paul alluded to two main aspects of the local church's worship, which divide the chapter in half. First he considered its scope and emphasized the need for a global concern in public worship (2:1-7), and second he considered its conduct and addressed the question of the respective roles of men and women in public worship (2:8-15).

Open
■ What role does worship play in your spiritual life?

in the life of your church body?

Study

■ In this pastoral letter Paul was looking beyond Timothy, to whom it is addressed, to the local churches he had been called to supervise. The apostle was concerned through Timothy to regulate the life of the church. He began with doctrine (chapter 1), urging Timothy to counter false teaching and to remain loyal to the apostolic faith. He continued with the conduct of public worship. *Read 1 Timothy 2:1-7.*

1. What kinds of prayer does Paul mention in this passage?

How do they differ from one another?

2. Paul began his instructions about public worship with prayer, stating that it is first in importance. Why is it so important?

3. Verse 2 tells us to pray "for kings and all those in authority." Who would be the equivalent of these people in your country today?

Why are you to pray for them?

Paul's instruction to pray for kings and all those in authority was remarkable since at that time no Christian ruler existed anywhere in the world. The reigning emperor was Nero, whose vanity, cruelty and hostility to the Christian faith were widely known. The persecution of the church, spasmodic at first, was soon to become systematic, and Christians were understandably apprehensive. Yet they had recourse to prayer. Indeed, prayer for pagan countries and their leaders already had a precedent in the Old Testament (Jeremiah 29:7; Ezekiel 6:10).

4. In linking prayer with salvation, what aspects of salvation did Paul highlight in verses 3-7?

5. How can we avoid both extremes of elitism (only some will be saved) and universalism (everybody will be saved) in reference to evangelism and salvation?

6. How is the truth about Jesus in verses 5 and 6 challenged today?

Summary: The first half of this chapter begins and ends with a reference to the church's worldwide responsibility. The local church has a global mission. According to verse 1 the church is to pray for all people; according to verse 7 it is to proclaim the gospel to all people, all nations. But how can the church be expected to include the whole world in the embrace of its intercession and its witness? Is not this perspective arrogant, presumptuous, even imperialistic? No! The universal concern of the church arises from the universal concern of God. It is because there is one God and one mediator that all people must be included in the church's prayers and proclamation. God's desire and Christ's death concern all people; therefore the church's duty concerns all people too, reaching out to them both in earnest prayer and in urgent witness.

Paul turned from the priority and scope of the local church's prayers to the respective roles and appropriate behavior of men and women whenever the church assembles for worship. *Read 1 Timothy 2:8-15.*

Verse 15 is rather ambiguous but may be best understood that "women will be saved through the Birth of the Child" (NEB), referring to Christ. Earlier in the chapter Jesus has been identified as "the one mediator," who of course became human by being "born of a woman" (Galatians 3:16).

---

8. This passage has been interpreted in a variety of ways and has caused numerous arguments about the roles of men and women in the church. One rule of interpretation is to determine universal instructions/principles and cultural expressions of them. Looking at verses 8-15 from this perspective, identify the universal instructions, cultural expressions in Paul's day and cultural expressions for today.

	Universal Instruction	Then	Now
verse 8			
verses 9-10			
verses 11-15			

---

9. Why did Paul focus on anger and disputing in connection with prayer?

10. How do the biblical reasons Paul cited support and explain his third instruction?

Summary: As men should pray in holiness, love and peace but not necessarily lift up their hands while they do so; and as women should adorn themselves with modesty, decency and good works but not necessarily abstain from all hair-braiding, gold and pearls; so women should submit to the headship (caring responsibility) of men and not try to reverse sexual roles, but not necessarily refrain from teaching men. If certain roles are not open to women, and even if they are tempted to resent their position, they and we must never forget what we owe to a woman. If Mary had not given birth to the Christ-child, there would have been no salvation for anybody.

Apply
■ What steps can you take to broaden the scope of your prayers?

How will the fact that God wants everyone to be saved affect how you interact with people this week?

If Paul were writing this letter to your church today, what might he say about the roles of men and women?

Pray
■ Ask God to provide opportunities for you to tell others about him this week and for the courage to speak up when they come.

4
A LEADER
TO FOLLOW

1 Timothy 3

*P*astor X Resigns His Church Because of Adultery"
"Rev. B Absconds with $200,000 of Church's Money"
When a pastor's moral or ethical sin becomes public, it also becomes news locally and sometimes nationally, depending on how well known the person is. Unbelievers take notice and judge Christianity and the church by the conduct of its leaders. In many ways a church's health and reputation largely depend on the quality, faithfulness and teaching of its ministers. So in this chapter, Paul turned to the pastoral oversight of the church and the necessary qualifications of pastors and deacons.

Open
■ What qualifications did you need for your current or a past job? Why?

Study
1. *Read 1 Timothy 3:1-7.* This passage begins with the second "trustworthy saying" in the pastoral epistles, focusing on the overseer, also called pastor

or elder. Why is being an overseer a "noble task"?

---

2. Paul lists a number of qualifications for pastor. Using this list, develop a questionnaire to give a potential pastor or elder. Include a definition or description of each qualification as well as an example.

---

3. Take a look at these qualifications, considering which are character qualities and which are abilities. Note why each is important for leaders.

Character Qualities   **Abilities**   **Importance**

Summary: Notice that these ten qualifications, for pastors focus primarily on character qualities and lifestyle conduct, not on specific duties. Because they emphasize character, they can also function as standards for other positions of leadership.

Read 1 Timothy 3:8-13. Since the Greek word for deacon means "a table waiter" and the verb form means "to engage in service of a social kind," deacons are thought to have specialized in practical administration and ministry. In light of the qualifications listed here, however, it is perhaps better to think of deacons as those who assist the overseers in their ministries.

4. From this list of qualifications for deacons, develop a second question-naire to use with potential candidates for this position. Include a definition or description of each qualification as well as an example.

Looking back, it is clear that the qualifications for the elders and deacons are very similar. There is a core of Christian qualities, which all Christian leaders should exhibit. Putting the two lists together, we note that there are five main areas to be investigated: self, family, relationships, treatment of outsiders and the faith.

---

5. Verse 11 literally begins "Women likewise." Commentators do not agree on whether these women are the deacons' wives or deaconesses, since the word can apply to either. What character qualities did Paul say they should possess?

---

6. Describe the reward for serving well as a deacon (v. 13).

In Greek society the deacon was one who gave lowly service, an act that was not considered dignified in a culture that valued ruling instead. But Jesus reversed this evaluation. "For who is greater," he asked, "the one who is at the table or the one who serves? Is it not the one who is at the table? But I am among you as one who serves" (Luke 22:27). And "even the Son of Man did not come to be served, but to serve" (Mark 10:45). It was from this teaching and example of Jesus that the general calling of all his followers to humble service derived.

From the qualifications for the pastorate, Paul turned to the church in which pastors serve. For the nature of the ministry is determined by the nature of the church. *Read 1 Timothy 3:14-16.*

7. How would you summarize Paul's purpose for writing this letter?

8. How did Paul describe the church?

What does each word picture convey about it?

9. In verse 16 Paul described Christ with a series of affirmations. What do they teach about him?

10. How do these statements build on one another?

Summary: Paul's perspective in this chapter is to view the pastors/elders and the deacons in the light of the church they are called to serve and to view the church in the light of the truth it is called to confess. One of the surest roads to the reform and renewal of the church is to recover its essential identity as "God's household, which is the church of the living God, the pillar and foundation of the truth" (v. 15).

Apply ————————————————————————

■ Think about the leadership roles you currently have (for example, parent, supervisor, committee chairperson). How do you measure up to the leadership qualifications listed in this chapter?

Which qualification do you want to cultivate or deepen in your life, and what specific steps will you take to do so?

Compare Paul's qualification lists with your church's qualifications for leaders. (See your church's constitution.) If they don't match, what can you do to encourage the leadership to make changes?

How can focusing on the description of Christ in verse 16 help you conduct yourself like God wants you to?

Pray ————————————————————————

■ Pray for God's working in your life to cultivate the leadership qualifications Paul mentioned in this chapter.

5
CHOOSE YOUR WEAPONS

1 Timothy 4:1—5:2

*T*rue or false? God is still adding to Scripture today.

True or false? A pastor who exercises too much control over the members of his congregation is a cult leader.

False teaching takes many forms. Sometimes it's easy for Christians to detect; other times it's so subtle we embrace it without realizing we've done so. Either way, it can destroy individual believers and churches. So Paul gave Timothy warnings and advice about false teachers and their lies. In this chapter, he first explained how to detect and expose false teaching; then he told how true teaching may be commended and endorsed in spite of Timothy's youth.

Open
■ What is the best advice you've received, and in what specific ways did it help you?

Study
1. *Read 1 Timothy 4:1-5.* What criteria for determining false teachers did Paul give in this passage?

2. The key statement in this paragraph is that in spite of the church's role as the guardian of the truth, "some will abandon the faith." The Greek word for abandon means "to apostatize." It was used of Israel's unfaithfulness to God in the Greek translation of the Old Testament. Why do people abandon their faith in God?

---

3. What contemporary false teachers do verses 1-3 describe?

---

4. Why is gratitude for what God has given us so important in fighting false teaching?

We should determine, then, to recognize and acknowledge all the gifts of the Creator: the glory of the heavens and the earth, of mountain, river and sea, of forest and flowers, of birds, beasts and butterflies, and of the intricate balance of the natural environment. We celebrate the unique privileges of our humanness (rational, moral, social and spiritual), as we were created in God's image and appointed his stewards; the joys of gender, marriage, sex, children, parenthood and family life, and of our extended family and friends. We appreciate the rhythm of work and rest, of daily work as a means to cooperate with God and serve the common good, and of the Lord's day when we exchange work for worship; the blessings of peace, freedom, justice and good government, and of food and drink, clothing and shelter; and our human creativity expressed in music, literature, painting, sculpture and drama, and in the skills and strengths displayed in sport.

---

5. *Read 1 Timothy 4:6-10.* What is our best defense against false teaching? Why?

6. How would you define *godliness*?

What are a couple of examples of how it is demonstrated in real life?

How then are we to train ourselves to be godly? What spiritual gymnastics are we to undertake? Paul does not go into detail. But the context and in particular the parallel between nourishment and exercise together suggest that we are to exercise ourselves in the same way that we nourish ourselves, namely in the Word of God. Certainly it has been a long-standing Christian tradition that disciplined meditation in Scripture is indispensable to Christian health and, indeed, to growth in godliness.

7. Verse 9 contains the third "trustworthy statement" in the pastoral letters. How does the truth of this saying help us combat false teaching?

Summary: Looking back over the first half of this chapter, we can now bring together the two tests that Paul gave Timothy and that can still be applied to doubtful teaching today. The theological test is the doctrine of creation: Does this teaching honor God as the creator and giver of all things? The second test is ethical and concerns the priority of godliness: Does this teaching honor God by drawing out our worship? We need have no hesitation about any teaching that glorifies God the Creator and promotes godliness.

8. *Read 1 Timothy 4:11—5:2.* Timothy had been called to Christian leadership beyond his years. His responsibility to "command and teach" was in danger of being undermined by his youthfulness and by the signs that his ministry was being rejected. How does Paul instruct him to live so that others will respect him?

9. When are you tempted to "neglect your gift"?

10. Paul told Timothy to "watch [his] life and doctrine closely." What is significant about the order of the words *life* and *doctrine?*

Summary: There is much practical wisdom here for everybody called to Christian leadership and especially for younger people given responsibility beyond their years. If they follow Paul's advice to Timothy, other people will not despise their youth but will gladly and gratefully receive their ministry.

Apply

■ What specific actions are you engaged in to train yourself to be godly so you won't succumb to false teaching?

What kind of example are you when measured against verse 12?

Which quality do you need to cultivate more of, and how will you do so this week?

Pray

■ What spiritual progress have people seen in you in the past few months? Spend a few minutes thanking God for the growth he has made in your life and asking for his help to continue to grow in godliness.

6
CARING FOR WIDOWS

1 Timothy 5:3-16

*S*ome say, "The church should preach the gospel, not get involved in social programs." While others say, "The church has a biblical responsibility to help people as well as witness to them." Christians position themselves on both sides of this debate and at points in between. The hot topic of social welfare in the church is not new, however. Paul had to deal with it in his first letter to Timothy.

Having just mentioned older and younger men and women in the Ephesian churches (5:1-2) and how Timothy should relate to them, in 5:3—6:2 Paul takes up three more particular groupings—widows, elders and slaves—and indicates what Timothy's and the churches' responsibilities are toward them. This study focuses on widows.

Open ───────────────────────────────

■ How much should the church be involved in social welfare like helping the homeless with shelter and food? Why?

Study ───────────────────────────────

■ Scripture has much to say about widows and honors them in a way that most cultures do not. Too often a married woman is defined only in relation to her husband. Then if he dies, she loses not only her spouse but her social significance as well. In Scripture, however, widows, orphans and aliens (people without husband, parents or home) are valued for who they are in themselves, and are said to deserve special honor, protection and care. Throughout the Bible justice and love are demanded for them. God is described as "a father to the fatherless" and "a defender of widows" (Psalm 68:5); and it is written of him that "he defends the cause of the fatherless and the widow" (Deuteronomy 10:18). Because this is the kind of God he is, his people are to be the same.

---

1. *Read 1 Timothy 5:3-8.* What qualifies a widow as one "in need" and thus deserving of support by the church?

Evidently the local church was maintaining some widows whose families should be supporting them. The legal provision of a dowry at marriage, provided by the bride's father, gave a widow financial security. She would be maintained out of her dowry either by her son or by her father. Such a widow did not need the church's support, since her own family had both a moral and a legal obligation to look after her.

---

2. How can we give "proper recognition" (v. 3) to widows in the church today?

Why should we do so?

---

3. When a widow "lives for pleasure" (v. 6), what does her lifestyle tell about her?

4. How is taking care of your family, including widows who are part of it, a testimony to others?

Here is an issue of considerable contemporary importance. As the medical care of the elderly improves, particularly in the West, the average age of the population continues to rise. There are many more old folk than ever before. Geriatric wards, homes and hospitals are full. And it is fine that the church and government should provide these, but not if it means that senior citizens are abandoned or neglected by their own relatives. Verse 8 tells us that it is a fundamental Christian duty to provide for our relatives. This is a plain biblical warrant for a life insurance policy.

The focus in verses 3-8 has been on the financial maintenance of widows, which in the first instance is the duty of their relatives and becomes the duty of the church only if the widow has no relatives. Verses 9-16 introduce new concerns.

5. *Read 1 Timothy 5:9-16.* According to this paragraph, the early church had a "register" or list of widows. What was the purpose of this list?

6. What are the qualifications for being on that list?

Why is each important?

7. Why don't younger widows qualify for this list?

Instead, what are younger widows to do?

Two lasting principles of social welfare emerge from these instructions. The first is the principle of discrimination. There was to be no general handout to all widows, irrespective of their circumstances. Instead, the church's welfare provisions are to be limited to those in genuine need. Second, there is the principle of dignity. Those who are able should serve others. Widows (together with others in similar circumstances like single mothers, abused and divorced women) should have the opportunity both to receive according to their need and to give according to their ability.

8. What general principles do the steps and qualifications outlined here teach us about offering care to people in need?

Apply ———————————————————————————————
■ How does your attitude toward widows, widowers and others in similar circumstances compare with Paul's?

How is your church taking care of needy members?

What specific things can you do to help?

Pray ———————————————————————————————
■ Pray that God will lead you to specific widows and others you can help. Ask him to help you make time and give up the provisions needed to do so.

7
SHOWING RESPECT

1 Timothy 5:17—6:2

W̶e sometimes say or think that Christian workers need the appreciation only of the Chief Shepherd and not of human leaders. But Paul was of a different opinion. For human beings are prone to discouragement and need to be affirmed.

In this section Paul addresses those who are worthy of respect. It is not surprising to see Christian leaders included here, but then Paul offers us a challenge: he says that slaveholders are "worthy of full respect." When one human being is forcibly owned by another, it is fundamentally destructive of that person's humanness. How then can we show honor to slaveowners?

Open

■ How do you feel when you know someone respects you?

How about when someone doesn't respect you?

Study

■ After addressing the care of widows, Paul turned to the church's treatment of elders and pastors. Having declared pastoral leadership to be "a noble task" (3:1) and having supplied a list of necessary qualifications (3:2-12), he moves on to practical issues.

1. *Read 1 Timothy 5:17-20.* What is the church's responsibility toward its elders?

2. In verse 18, how does Paul emphasize his point of appreciating an elder?

3. According to verses 19-20, how should a church handle accusations against an elder? (See also Deuteronomy 19:15.)

4. What will this procedure do to gossip?

Summary: The first issue in relation to elders that Paul dealt with was monetary appreciation. Appreciation may quite properly take a tangible, monetary form. Conscientious elders should receive both respect and remuneration, both honor and an honorarium. The second issue was fairness in discipline. He told Timothy to neither listen to frivolous accusations nor refuse to take serious situations seriously.

5. *Read 1 Timothy 5:21-25.* Paul then issued a charge to Timothy. What dangers did he tell Timothy to guard against in verse 21?

6. In verse 22 it is most likely that Paul is referring to ordination, which took place through the laying on of hands (see 1 Timothy 4:14; 2 Timothy 1:6). Why was it necessary for Paul to highlight this?

7. What seems to be the intent of the instruction in verse 23?

Verses 24 and 25 develop Paul's emphasis on the need for caution and give a further reason to avoid haste: human beings are frequently different from what they appear to be at first sight. They may seem initially either better or worse than they really are, for both their good and bad points may take a while to surface. So Timothy would need discernment.

8. How does each of these instructions apply to Timothy's position as pastor?

9. What impact do sins and good deeds have on others?

Summary: Here are five qualities that are needed by Christian leaders in their dealings with others they are responsible for: appreciation (affirming outstanding performance), fairness (not listening to unsubstantiated accusations), impartiality (avoiding all favoritism), caution (not reaching hasty decisions) and discernment (looking beyond the outward appearance to the heart). Whenever these principles are in operation, mistakes will be avoided, the church will be preserved in peace and love, and God's name will be protected from dishonor.

Having given Timothy instructions about the treatment of widows and elders, Paul then broached a third social relationship, namely the behavior of slaves toward their masters.

10. *Read 1 Timothy 6:1-2.* How should Christian slaves view their masters? Why?

11. Why should Christians work harder for other believers?

Summary: Every human being is worthy of honor, even pagan slave owners, because they have been made in the image of God. Once we perceive the intrinsic worth of humans by creation and therefore recognize them as worthy of honor, all our relationships are enriched and ennobled.

Apply
■ How well is your pastor cared for in these areas: respect, salary, fairness when accused?

What can you do to improve the situation in each area?

When do you find it difficult to show respect to those whom God said to respect?

How can you get past these barriers to obey God's instructions?

Pray
■ Pray that God will help you show respect to others, particularly your pastor and employer.

8
MONEY MATTERS

1 Timothy 6:3-21

*M*oney. It fosters sin. It furthers God's kingdom. It fuels debates. It divides believers. Some Christian groups teach a simple lifestyle with few material possessions, while others proclaim that God wants us to be rich and that success is measured by prosperity. Although Christians differ on their positions about money and how much we should accumulate, the trend today is toward having more rather than less.

Approximately 1,000 million inhabitants of this world are destitute, lacking the basic necessities for survival, while a small minority of people live in contrasting luxury. This disparity is not new; the early church struggled with the same issues. So Paul addressed the topic of money before concluding this letter to Timothy.

Open
■ What evidences of the love of money do you see among Christians today (both those who have money and those who lack it)?

Study
1. *Read 1 Timothy 6:3-5.* In contrast to "sound instruction," what characteristics and motives of false teachers did Paul focus on in these verses?

2. What are the results of their false teachings?

Summary: Looking back over these verses, we note that Paul has given us three practical tests by which to evaluate all teaching. We might put them in the form of questions: Is it compatible with the apostolic faith, that is, the New Testament? Does it tend to unite or divide the church? And does it promote godliness with contentment or covetousness?

3. Read 1 Timothy 6:6-10. Paul's word for contentment is the regular term used by the Stoics for a self-sufficiency that is altogether independent of circumstances. Christian contentment also does not depend on external things. How is godliness with contentment gain?

4. How does Paul argue for contentment and against greed?

5. What should be our attitude toward material things?

6. What is the price people pay for their love of money?

Summary: Paul's emphasis is clear, namely that covetousness is a self-destructive evil, whereas simplicity and contentment are beautiful and Christlike virtues. In a word, he is not for poverty against wealth but for contentment against covetousness.

Paul couched his next appeal, which is to Timothy himself, in poignant terms. He did not yet address him by name as he did in verse 20. Instead, he used the title of honor, "man of God." As a man of God,

Timothy was deliberately contrasted with the false teachers who were more men of the world than men of God.

---

7. *Read 1 Timothy 6:11-16.* What did Paul tell Timothy to do to combat covetousness? Give an example of each action.

Instruction   **Example**

---

8. What do you learn about God from Paul's supporting arguments for Timothy to keep this command?

Summary: It was natural for Paul, when he wrote about God, to break into a doxology, whether he was praising God for his mercy (as in 1:17) or for his power (as here). It was in the presence of this God, and in anticipation of his bringing about Christ's appearing, that Paul gave Timothy his solemn charge. Still today God's presence and Christ's appearing are two major incentives to faithfulness.

---

9. *Read 1 Timothy 6:17-19.* After a digression (vv. 11-16), Paul reverted to the topic of money. What are the dangers of being rich?

---

10. What obligations come with having wealth?

Summary: Looking over both paragraphs about money, the apostle's balanced wisdom becomes apparent. Against materialism (an obsession with material possessions) he set simplicity of lifestyle. Against asceticism (the repudiation of the material order) he set gratitude for God's creation.

Against covetousness (the lust for more possessions) he set contentment for what we have. Against selfishness (the accumulation of goods for ourselves) he set generosity in imitation of God. Simplicity, gratitude, contentment and generosity constitute a healthy balance for Christian living.

---

11. *Read 1 Timothy 6:20-21.* What was Paul's final charge to Timothy?

Why did he end that way?

Summary: In Paul's concluding prayer, "Grace be with you," the "you" is plural. It indicates Paul was looking beyond Timothy, as he has done throughout the letter, to the congregations he supervised. They would not be able in their own strength to reject error and fight for truth, to run from evil and pursue godliness, to renounce covetousness, and cultivate contentment and generosity, and in these Christian responsibilities to remain faithful to the end. Only divine grace could keep them. So at the letter's conclusion, as at its beginning (1:2), the apostle wished for them above all else an experience of the transforming and sustaining grace of God.

Apply ———————————————————————————————————
■ What practical steps can you take to flee materialism and follow godliness?

How can you use the wealth God has given you—whatever the amount—to do good works?

Pray ———————————————————————————————————
■ Pray that God will help you be a good steward of what he has given you.

9
TRUTH IN CHURCH

Titus 1

*D*eceivers, empty talkers, speculators, divisive controversialists and hypocritical liars were among the false teachers influencing the church. Paul was profoundly disturbed about the prevalence of false teaching. He refers to it in all his letters.

Paul refused to give in to the false teachers. Neither did he remain idle or silent on the ground that everybody has a right to his or her own opinion. And he did not secede from the church in the belief that it was irredeemable. So what was his strategy in fighting the good fight of the faith? It was this: when false teachers increase, we must multiply the number of true teachers. Titus was to appoint elders in every town who would hold fast to God's reliable word, teach it faithfully and refute those who contradicted it.

Open ───────────────────────────

■ On a scale of 1 to 10 (10 is highest), what score would your church, small group, Sunday-school class or fellowship group obtain in the area of practicing God's truth? Why?

Study ───────────────────────────

■ Like Timothy, Titus was entrusted with the care of churches to complete what Paul had started. After he accompanied Paul on his missionary journeys, Paul left him on the island of Crete with instructions to complete what had been left incomplete.

1. *Read Titus 1:1-4.* What does Paul's description of himself tell you about him?

2. Describe the "truth that leads to godliness" (v. 1).

Read Titus 1:5-9. In order to be sure God's truth continued in Crete, Paul told Titus to "appoint elders in every town" and described the kind of men to select. Although this list is similar to the one in 1 Timothy 3, the emphasis here is on blamelessness as the overriding requirement for eligibility for the pastorate. This does not mean, of course, that candidates must be flawless or faultless, or everyone would be disqualified. Instead, the Greek word used means "without blame" or "unaccused."

3. Paul emphasized that elders must be blameless in a number of areas. What are they?

4. Why is blamelessness so important for church leaders?

5. What positive qualities of elders are highlighted?

6. What functions or responsibilities of elders did Paul mention?

Neither of these responsibilities will be possible unless pastors maintain their firm hold on the sure word of the apostles, the "trustworthy message as it has been taught." This is the truth we now have in the New Testament.

7. *Read Titus 1:10-16.* Having given an ideal picture of true elders, Paul by contrast described the false teachers in Crete. How did he describe them?

8. What kind of influence do false teachers have?

Church fathers identified the author of the saying in verse 12 as the sixth-century B.C. Cretan teacher Epimenides of Knosses, who was held in high honor by his compatriots as both a prophet and a miracle-worker. His threefold estimate of the Cretan character was decidedly unflattering, but there seems to have been some confirmation of it. As for their reputation for lying, the Greeks coined both the verb for "lie" and the noun used for a "falsehood." As for being "evil beasts," Epimenides himself went further and joked that the absence of wild beasts on the island was supplied by its human inhabitants (Thomas Oden, *First and Second Timothy and Titus* [John Knox, 1989], p. 61).

9. How did Paul tell Titus to deal with the false teachers? Why?

10. According to verse 16, how can you determine whether someone truly knows God?

Summary: Looking back over this chapter within the context of the contemporary church, there are two major lessons we need to learn. First, let's copy Paul's strategy in relation to false teaching. When false teachers increase, we must multiply the number of true teachers. Second, let's maintain Paul's high standards of eligibility for pastors, particularly blamelessness. The church will be in a far healthier condition if we do.

Apply
■ Rate yourself according to the standards of leadership in this chapter. Are you blameless in your marriage and family life, character and conduct, and doctrinal orthodoxy? In what areas do you need to improve?

What specific steps will you take this week to become blameless in one of those areas?

Pray
■ Verse 16 says, "They claim to know God, but by their actions they deny him." Reflect on this before the Lord. Ask God to show you how this might be true of you.

10
TRUTH AT HOME

Titus 2

*B*ecause I told you" worked as an incentive to do something when we were young children who accepted everything our parents told us. But as we grew into teenagers, it was no longer a sufficient reason for changing our actions. We wanted to know *why* and needed a greater incentive.

Being the rational people we are as human beings, we need to know not only how we ought to behave as Christians, but also why. We certainly need instructions about the kind of people we ought to be, but we also need incentives. So what is Christian behavior? And what are its grounds? These questions belong to each other, and Titus 2 is an outstanding example of this double theme.

Open
■ What motivates you to change your behavior? Why?

Study
■ *Read Titus 2:1-10.* From the activities of false teachers, Paul turned to Titus's responsibilities as a true teacher. In fact the opening words of chapter

2, which the NIV did not translate, are "but as for you," emphasizing Titus's distinctive role in contrast to them. In this case, Titus was to behave in a way that is entirely unlike the false teachers. They professed to know God but denied him by their actions (1:16). They failed to practice what they preached. In Titus, however, there was to be no dichotomy in his teaching between belief and behavior. "But as for you," Paul wrote, "you must teach what is in accord with sound doctrine" (v. 1).

---

1. Paul gave specific instructions for five groups of people in addition to Titus. List each group along with what Paul told Titus to teach them.

	Group	**Teaching**
(v. 2)		
(vv. 3-4)		
(vv. 4-5)		
(v. 6)		
(vv. 7-8)		
(vv. 9-10)		

---

2. What instructions are given specifically for Titus?

We human beings seem to be imitative by nature. We need models; they give us direction, challenge and inspiration. Paul did not hesitate to offer himself, as an apostle, for the churches to imitate. "Follow my example," he wrote, "as I follow the example of Christ" (1 Corinthians 11:1). And Paul expected both Timothy and Titus to provide a model which the churches could follow.

3. Why did Paul give all of these instructions?

Three times in these verses about the Christian behavior of different groups, Paul highlighted his concern about the effect of the Christian witness on the non-Christian world. In two of them he referred to Christian doctrine which is salvation doctrine. So either we give no evidence of salvation, in which case the gospel is tarnished, or we give good evidence of salvation by living a manifestly saved life, in which the gospel shines. Our lives can bring either adornment or discredit to the gospel.

4. How do we draw unbelievers to the gospel and our Savior by the way we live?

5. What does your lifestyle reflect about your beliefs?

6. *Read Titus 2:11-15.* Paul moved on from duty to doctrine. His usual method was to begin with doctrine and then with a mighty "therefore" go on to its ethical implications. Here, however, the order is reversed. Paul began with ethical duties and, with a ringing "because," laid down their doctrinal foundation. Describe the doctrine which is highlighted here.

7. What behavior did Paul expect as a result of knowing this doctrine?

8. What is our motivation for godly living?

_____

How can this encourage us today?

_____

9. Why is teaching the truth so important?

_____

10. What charge did Paul give Titus? Why?

Apply
■ Find the group you belong to in verses 1-10. (Think of slaves as employees.) Which qualities do you need to learn?

_____

How can you begin to develop one of them this week?

_____

How can you help an older or younger Christian this week?

Pray
■ Pray that God will show you specific ways to make the gospel attractive to unbelievers and to follow through in helping an older or younger Christian this week.

11
TRUTH IN
THE WORLD

Titus 3:1-8

*T*he church is full of hypocrites."

"Christians aren't any different from the rest of us. So why should I want to become one?"

These two statements are major excuses people give for rejecting Christianity. Unfortunately, our behavior as Christians sometimes gives unbelievers cause for ignoring the salvation God offers. Paul dealt with this problem in the third chapter of Titus. Having given Titus directions about doctrine and duty in the church (chapter 1) and in the home (chapter 2), he then developed the same theme in regard to the world (chapter 3). Paul thus moved purposefully from the inner circles of home and church to the outer circle of secular society.

Open ———————————————————————
■ If someone followed you around for a week, how would that person describe your relationship with the world?

Study ———————————————————————
■ *Read Titus 3:1-2.* Paul began this section by telling Titus to "remind the

people" of something they already knew but apparently forgot—their social relationship in the world. The churches have heard it before. But there are many warnings in Scripture of the dangers of forgetfulness and many promises to those who remember.

---

1. How should we relate to rulers and others in authority over us? Give an example of each instruction.

---

2. Paul moved from our Christian responsibility toward the leaders of the community to our relationship with everybody in the community. How should we relate to unbelievers in general? Give an example of each action. (A sample is given to get you started.)

Action	Example
Do not slander (v. 2)	Don't tell others that your boss is having an affair just because he's friendly with a coworker.

---

3. Why are these instructions important?

Summary: The emphasis on "whatever is good" not only clarifies our responsibility to government but limits it. We cannot cooperate with the state if it reverses its God-given duty, promoting evil instead of punishing it and opposing good instead of rewarding and furthering it.

---

4. *Read Titus 3:3-8.* How is the person who does not know Christ described?

Paul gave a condensed but comprehensive account of salvation. Verses 4-7 are a single long sentence which he may have taken from an early Christian creed. The whole sentence hinges on the main verb "he saved us" (v. 5). It is perhaps the fullest statement of salvation in the New Testament. Yet whenever the phraseology of salvation is dropped into a conversation today, people's reactions are predictable. They will either blush, frown, snigger or even laugh, as if it were a huge joke. Thus the devil, whose ambition is to destroy, not to save, succeeds in trivializing the most serious question we could ever ask ourselves or put to anybody else. For Christianity is essentially a religion of salvation.

5. Why did God need to provide salvation for us?

6. According to these verses, how did he save us?

7. In these verses Paul is giving the theological reason we can expect Christians to have a social conscience and to behave responsibly in public life. The only reason we dare instruct others in social ethics is that we know what we were once like ourselves. Why is this important to recall?

8. Verse 8 begins with the fourth "trustworthy saying" of 1 and 2 Timothy and Titus. What is the content of this saying?

Why is it significant?

9. How can others know we are saved?

Summary: Note what a balanced and comprehensive account of salvation this is. For here are the three persons of the Trinity together engaged in securing our salvation: the love of God the Father, who took the initiative; the death of God the Son, in whom God's grace and mercy appeared; and the inward work of God the Holy Spirit, by whom we are reborn and renewed. Here too are the three tenses of salvation. The past is justification and regeneration. The present is a new life of good works in the power of the Spirit. The future is the inheritance of eternal life which will one day be ours.

Apply ───────────────────────────────────
■ How well do you live the instructions in verses 1 and 2 about relating to government authorities and unbelievers in general?

Do any of the actions in verse 3 still describe you? If so, what can you do this week to change your behavior in one area?

What evidences of salvation can others see in your lifestyle and motivations?

Pray──────────────────────────────────────
■ Thank God for his saving grace and ask for his help to live out your salvation in a way that attracts people to him.

12
UNITED WE STAND

Titus 3:9-15

*D*avid and his wife disagreed with almost everything their congregation did. When the education committee presented a new children's program, they argued against it, accusing ministry leaders of ignoring their offers to teach. When their philosophy of worship contradicted the worship committee's, they complained to everyone who would listen. When they weren't invited to serve in leadership positions, they grumbled to sympathetic listeners. Soon they had convinced a number of other families that the pastor and elders were out of line and consequently divided the congregation over a number of issues.

This problem is not new. In fact, Paul wrote about it in his concluding instructions to Titus.

Open
■ How do you respond to divisive people? Why?

Study
■ So far in Titus 3, Paul has done two things. First, he told Titus to remind the Christians in his care to be conscientious citizens and to live consistent

lives of peace, courtesy and gentleness. Whatever their national character or individual temperament, that is their calling. Second, Paul elaborated the doctrine of salvation and so gave Titus a ground for confidence that the people in his charge can be changed so as to live the new life to which they were summoned.

Paul concluded his letter with a cluster of miscellaneous messages with requests or instructions for Titus to do something.

---

1. *Read Titus 3:9-15.* After telling Titus to stress the truth of salvation (v. 8), the apostle then told him to avoid other things. What errors did Paul say to avoid? Give an example of each.

---

2. Why is it important to avoid these?

---

3. Paul then gave specific instructions regarding a divisive person. Define and describe such a person.

---

4. How are we to treat divisive people? Why?

---

5. How did Paul want Titus to help him (vv. 12-15)?

---

6. What do his instructions indicate about their relationship?

As Paul ended this letter, he mentioned a number of people by name. Of Artemas we know nothing. Tychicus came from proconsular Asia, perhaps from Ephesus, its capital, like Trophimus, with whom he was bracketed. He was one of those chosen to take the collection for the poor to Jerusalem. Paul called him a "dear brother and faithful servant in the Lord" (Ephesians 6:21) and evidently had great confidence in him. He sent him to Colosse, perhaps with his letter to tell the churches about him. Later Paul sent him from Rome to Ephesus to free Timothy to go visit him.

We know nothing of Zenas except that Paul called him a lawyer. Apollos may well be the learned and eloquent Alexandrian who had "a thorough knowledge of the Scriptures" (Acts 18:24) and who exercised a fruitful ministry in Corinth. It seems likely that Paul had entrusted to these two men the task of carrying his letter to Titus on Crete.

---

7. Why are believers to learn to devote themselves to good works?

---

8. Why did Paul emphasize greeting "those who love us in the faith"?

---

9. How do the actions Paul encourages here contrast with the actions he condemns in verses 9-11?

---

10. What is the relationship between God's grace in salvation and in our good works?

Summary: Having now studied the three chapters that make up this short letter, it is evident that "doctrine and duty" is an appropriate title for it. For in the church (chapter 1) Christian leaders, in contrast to false teachers, are to pass on the apostolic faith and practice what they preach. In the home (chapter 2) members of the household are to go about their different duties in this present age, motivated by the past and future appearances of Christ. And in the world (chapter 3) conscientious Christian citizenship is to be a spontaneous overflow of that great salvation which God—Father, Son and Holy Spirit—has won for us.

Thus doctrine inspires duty, and duty adorns doctrine. Doctrine and duty are married; they must not be divorced.

Apply

■ How can you guard against becoming a divisive person?

Evaluate yourself in relation to good works. In what specific ways can you live a more productive life?

Paul wrote to both Timothy and Titus to encourage them as well as to instruct them. Who can you write to this week to practice the truth?

What is the most important truth you learned from the book of Titus? Why?

Pray

■ Pray that your attitudes and actions will bring unity, not divisiveness, to your church. Ask God to help you continue to live out the truths you've learned from this study.

Guidelines for Leaders

My grace is sufficient for you. (2 Corinthians 12:9)

If leading a small group is something new for you, don't worry. These sessions are designed to be led easily. Because the Bible study questions flow from observation to interpretation to application, you may feel as if the studies lead themselves.

You don't need to be an expert on the Bible or a trained teacher to lead a small group discussion. As a leader, you can guide group members to discover for themselves what the Bible has to say and to listen for God's guidance. This method of learning will allow group members to remember much more of what is said than a lecture would.

This study guide is flexible. You can use it with a variety of groups—students, professionals, neighborhood or church groups. Each study takes forty-five to sixty minutes in a group setting.

There are some important facts to know about group dynamics and encouraging discussion. The suggestions listed below should equip you to effectively and enjoyably fulfill your role as leader.

Preparing for the Study

1. Ask God to help you understand and apply the passage in your own life. Unless this happens, you will not be prepared to lead others. Pray too for the various members of the group. Ask God to open your hearts to the message of his Word and motivate you to action.

2. Read the introduction to the entire guide to get an overview of the topics that will be explored.

3. As you begin each study, read and reread the assigned Bible passage to familiarize yourself with it.

4. This study guide is based on the New International Version of the Bible. It will help you and the group if you use this translation as the basis for your study and discussion.

5. Carefully work through each question in the study. Spend time in meditation and reflection as you consider how to respond.

6. Write your thoughts and responses in the space provided in the study guide. This will help you to express your understanding of the passage clearly.

7. You may want to get a copy of the Bible Speaks Today commentary by John Stott that supplements the Bible book you are studying. The commentary is divided into short units on each section of Scripture so you can easily read the appropriate material each week. This will help you answer tough questions about the passage and its context.

It may help to have a Bible dictionary handy. Use it to look up any unfamiliar words, names or places. (For additional help on how to study a passage, see *How to Lead a LifeGuide Bible Study* from InterVarsity Press, USA.)

8. Take the "Apply" portion of each study seriously. Consider how you need to apply the Scripture to your life. Remember that the group members will follow your lead in responding to the studies. They will not go any deeper than you do.

Leading the Study

1. Begin the study on time. Open with prayer, asking God to help the group to understand and apply the passage.

2. Be sure that everyone in your group has a study guide. Encourage the group to prepare beforehand for each discussion by reading the introduction to the guide and by working through the questions in each study.

3. At the beginning of your first time together, explain that these studies are meant to be discussions, not lectures. Encourage the members of the group to participate. However, do not put pressure on those who may be hesitant to speak during the first few sessions.

4. Have a group member read aloud the introduction at the beginning of the discussion.

5. Every session begins with an "open" question, which is meant to be asked before the passage is read. These questions are designed to introduce the theme of the study and encourage group members to begin to open up. Encourage as many members as possible to participate, and be ready to get the discussion going with your own response.

These opening questions can reveal where our thoughts or feelings need to be transformed by Scripture. That is why it is especially important not to read the passage before the question is asked. The passage will tend to color the honest reactions people would otherwise give because they are, of course, supposed to think the way the Bible does.

6. Have a group member read aloud the passage to be studied.

7. As you ask the study questions, keep in mind that they are designed to be used just as they are written. You may simply read them aloud. Or you may prefer to express them in your own words.

There may be times when it is appropriate to deviate from the study guide. For example, a question may have already been answered. If so, move on to the next question. Or someone may raise an important question not covered in the guide. Take time to discuss it, but try to keep the group from going off on tangents.

8. Avoid answering your own questions. If necessary repeat or rephrase them until they are clearly understood. Or point the group to the commentary woven into the guide to clarify the context or meaning without answering the question. An eager group quickly becomes passive and silent if members think the leader will do most of the talking.

9. Don't be afraid of silence in response to the discussion questions. People may need time to think about the question before formulating their answers.

10. Don't be content with just one answer. Ask, "What do the rest of you think?" or "Anything else?" until several people have given answers to the question.

11. Acknowledge all contributions. Try to be affirming whenever possible. Never reject an answer. If it is clearly off-base, ask, "Which verse led you to that conclusion?" or again, "What do the rest of you think?"

12. Don't expect every answer to be addressed to you, even though this will probably happen at first. As group members become more at ease, they will begin to truly interact with each other. This is one sign of healthy discussion.

13. Don't be afraid of controversy. It can be very stimulating. If you don't resolve an issue completely, don't be frustrated. Explain that the group will move on and God may enlighten all of you in later sessions.

14. Periodically summarize what the group has said about the passage. This helps to draw together the various ideas mentioned and gives continuity to the study. But don't preach.

15. Conclude your time together with conversational prayer, adapting the prayer suggestion at the end of the study to your group. Ask for God's help in following through on the commitments you've made.

16. End on time.

Many more suggestions and helps can be found in *How to Lead a LifeGuide Bible Study* and *The Big Book on Small Groups* (both from InterVarsity Press, USA) and *Housegroups* (Crossway Books, UK). Reading through one of these books would be worth your time.

For Further Reading
from InterVarsity Press

The Bible Speaks Today by John Stott
The books in this practical and readable series are companions to the John Stott
Bible Studies. They provide further background and insight into the passages.

The Message of Acts
The Message of Ephesians
The Message of Galatians
The Message of Romans (UK title), *Romans,* (US title)
The Message of the Sermon on the Mount (Matthew 5—7)
The Message of 1 & 2 Thessalonians
The Message of 1 Timothy & Titus (UK title), *Guard the Truth* (US title)
The Message of 2 Timothy